Care for your

Puppy

Tina Hearne

Contents

Record Card   2
Choosing a Puppy   3
Pedigree Puppies   4-5
Non-pedigree Puppies   6
Which Sex?   7
Size   8-9
Biology   10-11
Feeding   12-13
Housing   14-15
Varieties   16-17
Exercise   18-19
Grooming   20-1
Basic Training   22-3
Vaccination   24-5
The Healthy Puppy   26
Life History   27
Ailments   28-9
Responsible Ownership   30-1
Index   32

Acknowledgements

Animal Photography,
RSPCA/Sue Streeter, Solitaire/Tony Stone Worldwide

Illustrations by Terry Riley/David Lewis Artists and Robert Morton

First published in 1985
4 5 6 7 8 9

Published by William Collins Sons & Company Limited
London   Glasgow . Sydney . Auckland . Toronto . Johannesburg
© Royal Society for the Prevention of Cruelty to Animals 1985
Printed in Italy by New Interlitho, Milan
ISBN 0 00 410212 6

Collins

Record Card

Record sheet for your own puppy

Name

Date of birth
(actual or estimated)

photograph or portrait

Breed   Sex

Colour/description

Licence number   Annual renewal date

Feeding notes   Medical record (date of first season/date of neutering operation/
                                    dates of veterinary treatment for worming, vaccinations, etc.)

Veterinary surgeon's name   Surgery hours

Practice address   Tel. no.

Choosing a Puppy

It is necessary to resist impulse buying when choosing a puppy, and instead to think carefully about the sort of dog you want and whether it will fit happily into the kind of home and lifestyle you have to offer. One important consideration is that of cost. Quite apart from obvious expense such as the initial purchase price, the cost of the kennel and its accessories, and the mounting cost of feeding as the puppy grows bigger, there are always unexpected expenses such as additional veterinary treatment. Even the routine veterinary treatment (worming, vaccination, a neutering operation) can be expensive, but such expenditure must be anticipated as part of the overall expense of taking a puppy into the family.

Puppies can be irresistible. With their beguiling faces and their trusting ways they are often the victims of impulse buying, only to be cruelly abandoned later, or brought to the RSPCA for rehoming or destruction.

Our Stone Age ancestors were the first to succumb to the puppies' charm. It is thought that it was the puppies of the wild dogs which, ten thousand years ago, ingratiated themselves with early man by begging for food around the settlement camp fire. It is not difficult to imagine, perhaps, a litter of abandoned puppies, made bold by hunger, being rewarded with a few bones and scraps. In this way, it is suggested, the dog became the first animal to be domesticated (indeed, the only animal to be domesticated for four thousand years). The long history of man's remarkable relationship with the dog, as devoted hunting companion and guard, now gives it a unique position among the animals kept as pets.

Before buying a puppy, please make quite certain that you are able to offer it a suitable home: not just a house and garden of the right dimensions for the size and temperament of the puppy in mind, but a stable environment. Many young puppies suffer stress as a result of family arguments, for example. They can also be made most anxious by the arrival of a new spouse, or a new baby. When puppies are badly affected by such traumas they can develop a whole range of neurotic symptoms, including excessive licking, self-mutilation, howling and barking when alone, destruction of property and so on.

The best approach is to consult your veterinary surgeon *before* buying a puppy. He or she can give extensive advice about the sort of puppy that might be suitable for your own circumstances, and an early veterinary examination before the sale is finalized can reveal most hereditary disorders (p. 5) and will ensure you buy a sound and healthy animal.

Good breeders will accept a post-dated cheque for a puppy to allow time for such an examination.

Pedigree Puppies

Not all pedigree puppies will grow into suitable family pets, for each breed was originally evolved to fulfil a purpose for which its inherent qualities of speed, size, stamina, conformation and temperament are well suited.

Hounds Hounds were bred to hunt other animals (shown here in brackets) either by sight or by scent. Examples of sight hounds are the Afghan (leopard), Borzoi (wolf), Greyhound (hare and deer), Irish Wolf-hound (wolf), Rhodesian Ridgeback (lion) and Saluki (gazelle). All are long-legged and swift.

Scent hounds, by contrast, are short-legged and well adapted to follow a trail by scent. They include the Basset Hound, Beagle and Bloodhound. Hounds have both the instinct and stamina to range wide over the countryside.

Afghan Hound

Terriers These are the smallest of the hunting breeds. They take their name from the Latin word *terra*, meaning earth, for they work by going to earth themselves to bolt their quarry. As so many of the breed names suggest – Airedale, Border, Irish, Kerry Blue, Lakeland, Scottish, Skye, Welsh, West Highland, etc. – they were kept throughout the country on large estates and farms to control vermin, badgers, foxes and otters. By nature tough, energetic, loyal and fearless, those terriers which adapt to pet life are valued as lively companions and reliable house dogs, but may be aggressive with strangers.

Fox Terrier

Gundogs These breeds are trained to assist man in finding, pointing and retrieving game birds and water-fowl, whether from land or from water. Because their traditional role is not to kill but to co-operate, they are obedient and dependable. Gundogs include Setters, Pointers, Retrievers and Spaniels. Of these, the Golden Retriever and Labrador Retriever probably adapt to pet life better than any other sporting breeds, but their superb natures should not be abused by lack of exercise.

American Cocker Spaniel

German Shepherd Dog

Shih Tzu

Chihuahua

Working dogs   These include the breeds trained to herd sheep and cattle, e.g. the Collie, German Shepherd Dog, Old English Sheepdog, Pyrenean Mountain Dog, Shetland Sheepdog and Welsh Corgi; those bred to guard people, property and animals, e.g. the Boxer, Bull Mastiff, Dobermann, Great Dane and Rottweiler; those polar breeds used for drawing sleighs, e.g. the Alaskan Malamute, Samoyed and Siberian Husky; and the two famous rescue breeds, the St Bernard and the Newfoundland. All are country dogs, and must not be kept too confined.

Utility dogs   Utility dogs are those breeds not included in the sporting or working categories above, yet which were once bred to a particular role (shown here in brackets), although most are now successfully kept as pets. Notable members of this group are the Bulldog (bull-baiting), Chow Chow (bred for fur and meat in the East), Dalmatian (carriage escort dog), Keeshond (Dutch barge dog), Poodle (performing dog bred from a water retriever) and Shih Tzu (lion dog of China).

Toy dogs   These include miniature versions of the larger breeds and have been bred as lapdogs or for the show bench. They are inexpensive to feed, need little exercise and have many devotees among those who like a constant companion about the house. However, selective breeding for small size has rendered them, as a group, delicate and rather excitable. Well-known toy breeds are the Chihuahua, Maltese, Papillon, Pekingese, Pomeranian, Pug and Yorkshire Terrier.

Not only the toy breeds suffer hereditary defects. Centuries of inbreeding have weakened many breeds, making them prone to such defects as cataracts, deafness, haemophilia, elongated soft palates, epilepsy, hip dysplasia, hernias, progressive retinal atrophy and many more. Early veterinary examination (p. 3) is recommended.

Non-pedigree Puppies

One million puppies are estimated to be born in the United Kingdom every year. A large number of these – perhaps 650,000 – are born as a result of accidental or casually arranged matings. Puppies of unplanned pregnancies are usually crossbreds or mongrels and tend, for genetic reasons, to be physically more robust and temperamentally more stable than some inbred pedigree puppies.

Crossbred puppies

Crossbreds are the puppies born to purebred parents of different breeds. The puppies will inherit half their genes from the dam, half from the sire. As the genes control all the myriad characteristics of size, shape, colour, coat type and so on, as well as intelligence and temperamental traits, the resulting puppies will show a combination of both parents' looks and temperaments, and can be highly attractive. It should be said here, however, that if an accidental mating or 'misalliance' is discovered, pregnancy can be prevented providing the bitch is taken to a veterinary surgeon for an injection within 72 hours, and preferably within 24 hours.

Yorkshire Terrier/Cavalier King Charles Spaniel cross

Mongrel puppies

Mongrel puppies are those of mixed ancestry and no definable breed. When breeding pedigree puppies the choice of parents (and therefore of genetic material) is strictly limited; with the mongrel population the choice is unlimited. This accounts for the diversity, strength and hardiness of mongrel puppies, and for their relative lack of inherited and congenital disorders. They can make delightful pets.

It is sometimes possible to adopt a puppy from an animal welfare society such as the local branch of the RSPCA (as listed in the telephone directory), which will welcome enquiries from responsible adults. RSPCA personnel take great trouble to check that the home offered is suitable for a chosen puppy.

Mongrel

Which Sex?

The spaying operation is for the surgical removal of the ovaries (ovarectomy) or ovaries and uterus (ovari-hysterectomy), preferably 2–3 months after the cessation of the first season. The success rate is very high, and a tendency towards obesity, which can be a side-effect, can be controlled easily by monitoring any weight gain and reducing food intake accordingly.

Female

Most female puppies can be expected to reach puberty at about 8 months of age when they will normally have their first oestrus or season (p. 27). Subsequently, they will have a season every 6 months, each lasting for 3 weeks. At these times the bitch will be attractive to dogs which will seek her out, follow her on walks and attempt to mate her, and gather round the house howling. The bitch herself may have a change of temperament, becoming lethargic or, conversely, highly excitable; her bleeding can stain carpets and furnishings; and some people are embarrassed by the sight of her constantly cleaning herself.

For these reasons, but mostly because of the high risk of pregnancy, most owners seek to control oestrus. Some pen up the bitch, or board her at kennels; some attempt control by deodorant sprays; some use prescribed hormonal treatment. The RSPCA recommends the surgical control of oestrus in pet bitches by spaying.

Male

A male puppy can be expected to reach maturity at between 8 and 12 months, by which time he will be displaying characteristic male dog behaviour. This may include wandering off in search of bitches; attempting to mate any bitches encountered or even, when frustrated, cushions, cats, and people; and becoming aggressive with other dogs or with people. He will also spray urine to mark territory. Such behaviour can be worrying, dangerous, and embarrassing. For these reasons, but also to prevent their dogs being responsible for unwanted litters, many owners have their dogs castrated. Castration, which is the surgical removal of the testes, renders a dog sterile. It is also used as a means of controlling sexual behaviour. Your veterinary surgeon will advise as to whether castration or medicinal control is appropriate for your own pet dog.

Pair of Cocker Spaniels

Size

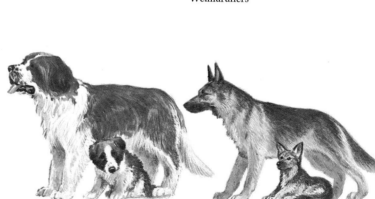

Giant Breeds
36–84 kg/80–185 lb

Bloodhounds
Deerhounds
Great Danes
Mastiffs and Bull Mastiffs
Newfoundlands
Pyrenean Mountain Dogs
St Bernards (illustrated)
Irish Wolfhounds

Large Breeds
23–36 kg/50–80 lb

Afghan Hounds
Borzois
Dobermanns
German Shepherd Dogs
 (illustrated)
Giant Schnauzers
Greyhounds
Irish Setters
Old English Sheepdogs
Rhodesian Ridgebacks
Rottweilers
Salukis
Weimaraners

175 cm

150 cm

125 cm

100 cm

75 cm

50 cm

25 cm

Scale

Dogs vary in size more than any other pet animal. In height they range from the Irish Wolfhound, standing 81 cm/32 in at the shoulder, down to the Yorkshire Terrier, standing only 20 cm/8 in.

The weight range is just as great. The Chihuahua weighs perhaps 1 kg/2 lb, the St Bernard 70 kg/150 lb, and mongrels can be as much as 36 kg/80 lb. Size, then, is an important consideration all too often ignored when choosing a dog. For some reason people will not accept

Medium Breeds
13.5–23 kg/30–50 lb

Basset Hounds
Boxers
Bulldogs
Chow Chows
Collies, Bearded Collies, and
    Border Collies
Dalmations
Keeshonds
Pointers and German Pointers
Poodles (Standard), (illustrated)
Retrievers (including Labradors)
Samoyeds
Spaniels (Clumber, Field,
    English and Welsh
    Springer, Sussex, Irish
    Water)
Terriers (Airedale, Irish, Kerry
    Blue, Soft-Coated Wheaten)

Small Breeds
4.5–13.5 kg/10–30 lb

Basenjis
Beagles
Bull Terriers, and Staffordshire
    Bull Terriers
Dachshunds
French Bulldogs
Poodles (Miniature)
Schipperkes
Schnauzers and Miniature
    Schnauzers
Shetland Sheepdogs
Shih Tzu
Spaniels (Cocker and American
    Cocker)
Terriers (except those listed as
    medium or toy)
    (Scottish Terrier illustrated)
Welsh Corgis
Whippets

Toy Breeds
1 –4.5 kg/2 –10 lb

Cavalier King Charles Spaniels
Chihuahuas (illustrated)
English Toy Terriers
Griffons Bruxellois
Italian Greyhounds
Japanese Chin
King Charles Spaniels
Maltese
Miniature Pinschers
Papillons
Pekingese
Pomeranians
Pugs
Silky Terriers
Yorkshire Terriers

6 ft —

5 ft —

4 ft —

3 ft —

2 ft —

1 ft —

how much small puppies can grow.

For ordinary family life, dogs from the small and middle ranges do best. Most are physically robust, and fit with reasonable comfort into a family-sized house and car, enabling them to accompany their owners on most outings.

As a general rule, the large breeds are remarkably tolerant of children and good guard dogs too, but they do need much more space.

Biology

Stance An example of good stance is illustrated, but selective breeding has produced many variations, which can predispose to certain disorders.

The hind limbs The crouching stance of the German Shepherd Dog is achieved because its hind limbs are in permanent flexion, resulting in a sloping spine and exacerbating the possibility of posterior paralysis and hip dysplasia. In contrast, the overextension of the hind limbs of taller dogs, such as Great Danes and Newfoundlands, can cause the stifle joint to dislocate backwards.

The fore limbs The enormous width of the chest of the Bulldog can cause the fore limbs to bow, resulting in uneven wear on the joints. The long-backed, short-legged breeds such as Dachshunds may also have bowed fore limbs and splayed-out toes. Both problems can result in arthritis.

Head and eyes Selective breeding has resulted in variations ranging from the elongated eyes of the long-nosed dogs such as the Greyhound and Collie, to the protuberant eyes of short-faced breeds such as the Pug and Pekingese (illustrated). Certain disorders are associated.

In general, the long-nosed dogs suffer fewer disadvantages than the short-faced breeds. The short-nosed dogs can suffer breathing difficulties, overcrowded teeth, and eczema in the folds of skin. The protuberant eyes, just by their prominence, are predisposed to irritation and accidental damage that may give rise to corneal ulcers. They also flatten and distort the tear ducts so that, instead of draining into the nose, tears tend to run down the cheeks. Another problem is that protuberant eyes can prolapse out of their sockets.

Genitalia There is an increasing number of male pedigree puppies whose testicles do not descend into the scrotal sac normally. At the time of purchase, it may be found that the puppy has only one testicle in the scrotum – or even none. This is usually a hereditary defect, and it is reprehensible in law to sell such a puppy without drawing attention to the condition.

The undescended testicle can sometimes be located in the groin. If not, then it is inside the abdominal cavity. Quite often it will descend at a later date, but if after 6 months this has not occurred, it is unlikely to do so. Unfortunately, such a condition can lead to serious problems from middle age onwards.

It is not possible to judge whether the development and function of the female sex organs are satisfactory until the puppy has her first season (p. 7). This is one reason for not spaying too early. Another is that spaying before skeletal growth is complete may leave the bitch with a permanent infantile vulva predisposed to pruritis (severe itching).

Short-faced Pekingese

Milk teeth Most puppies are born toothless, although the outline of the teeth can be seen in the gums. By the time the puppy is bought at 8 weeks, it will have a full set of deciduous, or milk teeth. Indeed, many puppies will have cut them all by the age of 4 weeks.

A full set of milk teeth comprises 3 incisors at the front, then 1 canine, and 3 premolars at the back on each side of the upper jaw, and the same for the lower jaw. This gives a total of 28 teeth.

The 3rd premolars and canines erupt before the incisors, which are cut in succession (from the sides towards the centre of the mouth), and those in the upper jaw appear before those in the lower jaw. The 1st and 2nd premolars are the last to erupt.

Puppies lose their deciduous teeth between 2 and 4 months.

Permanent teeth A full set of permanent teeth comprises, in the upper jaw, 3 incisors at the front, then 1 canine, 4 premolars and 2 molars on each side, and in the lower jaw, 3 incisors, 1 canine, 4 premolars, and 3 molars on each side. This gives a total of 42 teeth.

There is considerable variation, but in general big dogs teethe before the toy breeds. Between 2 and 5 months of age, the permanent upper front incisors erupt, then the lower incisors, followed by the premolars. The canines are usually through by the age of 6 months. Last to appear are the permanent molars, but even these are in place and dentition is complete by the age of 8 months.

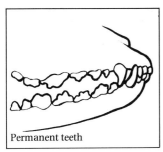

Permanent teeth

Teething Some puppies have trouble teething. They may have a gum infection or, more often, sore gums and persistent milk teeth. Gum infections will need veterinary treatment, but chewing on a large marrow bone, or a manufactured dog chew, will help to relieve soreness and complete the shedding of the milk teeth.

If the deciduous canines are not shed in time, it may be necessary to have them extracted. If not, they can either cause the permanent canines to be displaced, or cause them to decay as a result of food being trapped between the persistent milk canines and the newly erupting permanent teeth.

Claws A puppy's nails should not be clipped while it is very young. Once allowed out, after vaccination (p. 24), the puppy will usually wear down its own claws naturally by exercising on hard ground and pavements. If clipped before this, there is a tendency for the claws to lose their curvature and grow straight.

Split and fractured claws, damaged by the exuberant play of puppies, can cause bleeding and tenderness, and sometimes infection of the nail-bed, all of which need veterinary attention.

Dewclaws Puppies are born with dewclaws on the fore limbs, and 20–30 per cent also have dewclaws on the hind limbs. The front ones seldom give trouble, but the hind ones tend to get torn and may bleed profusely.

Although any mutilation is questionable on ethical grounds, many veterinary surgeons feel that, to avoid trauma, it is preferable to remove the hind dewclaws at the age of 3–5 days. There are certain exceptions. For instance, the breed standard for Pyrenean Mountain Dogs requires that the hind dewclaws should be retained.

Ears A puppy with erect ears is less likely to suffer ear trouble than a puppy with folded ears. Folded ears prevent good ventilation of the ear canal not only by obstructing its entrance, but also by distorting the canal further by their sheer weight.

Debris such as dust, grit, grass seeds and wax accumulates and is trapped in a folded ear, predis-posing to a variety of infections caused by anaerobic bacteria which thrive in such an environment.

Woolly-coated dogs such as Poodles, which do not moult, need to have the hair in the ear canal plucked regularly to increase the circulation of air and to prevent the accumulation of debris.

Ear cropping is one mutilation that is thankfully not carried out in the UK, but in certain European countries, for example, some breeds may still have their ears cropped (i.e. cut) to 'improve' their outline.

Spaniel with docked tail

Tail docking The RSPCA opposes the practice of tail docking for cosmetic, i.e. non-veterinary, reasons.

At present, under UK law a puppy may be docked without anaesthetic before its eyes open. The mutilation is usually carried out when the puppy is 3–5 days old in order to conform to the breed standards. These are quite arbitrary. For instance, Pembroke Corgis are docked, but not Cardiganshire Corgis.

Docking causes the puppy pain, however short-lived, yet local anaesthetic is not used because it can present another danger to such a young puppy.

Unfortunately, not all puppies are docked by veterinary surgeons. Incorrect docking may give rise to short-term or permanent damage: stump infection with possible necrosis or even gangrene; incontinence as a result of partial paralysis of the nerve supply to the sphincter muscles of the anus and the rectal wall; neuritis at the nerve ending, causing the puppy to chase its 'tail' and chew the stump; and even neuroma, which is a tumour on the severed nerve ending.

Scottie with pricked ears

Feeding

The balanced diet

The constituents of a balanced diet are protein, fat, carbo-hydrate, vitamins, minerals, water and roughage.

Protein (meat, offal, fish, and occasionally cheese and eggs) must account for a considerable proportion of the diet. Meat and fish fit for human consumption may be fed raw; offals should be cooked and fed only in moderation.

Carbohydrate is obtained from such cereal foods as biscuit and biscuit meal, wholemeal bread and, for young pup-pies, puppy meal, cooked rice, baby cereals and porridge.

Fat is obtained from the protein foods and from milk.

Extra vitamins and minerals should be given to puppies in a calcium-rich mineral/vitamin supplement.

Roughage is provided by cereal foods and vegetables. As dogs synthesize vitamin C, greens need not be given.

Fresh drinking water must always be within reach.

The puppy at 2–4 months

Whenever possible, follow the breeder's feeding notes while the 8-week-old puppy is settling in to its new home, and make changes only gradually. Such very young puppies need food that is easy to digest, and so minced meat (particularly white meat), flaked fish, cooked cereal foods (see above) and milk are important constituents of the diet. At this age the puppy will need four regular meals a day: milk and cereal at 8 a.m.; meat and cereal at noon; milk and cereal at 4 p.m.; and meat and cereal at 8 p.m. Avoid feeding milk and meat together.

The puppy at 4–10 months

As the puppy grows, the number of meals given is reduced, while the amount of food offered at each is increased. At 4 months omit one of the milk and cereal meals; at 6 months omit the other. At this time begin to offer a dish of milk separately. By 10 months, only small breeds will need two meals a day. Larger breeds will thrive on one main meal and one much smaller meal.

Convenience foods   If tinned meat is to be given, it is recommended that it be introduced into the diet progressively from the age of 4 months. Some varieties contain a mixture of proteins and carbohydrates with supplements, and these brands are designed to meet all the nutritional needs. Others contain meat intended to be fed with cereal such as biscuit or biscuit meal. When additional cereal is indicated, feed an equal volume of cereal and tinned food.

Dried foods are also intended to provide for all the nutritional needs. However, they have the disadvantage of monotony and may create increased thirst in the puppy which must be satisfied by the provision of a generous supply of fresh drinking water.

In all cases follow the manufacturer's advice about quantities, always allowing for individual variation between puppies.

GUIDE TO THE DAILY FEEDING OF PUPPIES
(allow for individual variation)

Type of breed & ADULT weight	Age (months)	Meat (weight when raw)	Milk (maximum quantity)
Toy: up to 4.5 kg (10 lb)	2–4	30–60 g (1–2 oz)	70 ml ($\frac{1}{8}$ pt)
	4–6	60–85 g (2–3 oz)	110 ml ($\frac{1}{5}$ pt)
	6–9	85–110 g (3–4 oz)	140 ml ($\frac{1}{4}$ pt)
Small: 4.5–13.5 kg (10–30 lb)	2–4	60–110 g (2–4 oz)	140 ml ($\frac{1}{4}$ pt)
	4–6	110–170 g (4–6 oz)	140 ml ($\frac{1}{4}$ pt)
	6–9	170–225 g (6–8 oz)	140 ml ($\frac{1}{4}$ pt)
Medium: 13.5–23 kg (30–50 lb)	2–4	85–170 g (3–6 oz)	280 ml ($\frac{1}{2}$ pt)
	4–6	170–250 g (6–9 oz)	280 ml ($\frac{1}{2}$ pt)
	6–9	250–335 g (9–12 oz)	280 ml ($\frac{1}{2}$ pt)
Large: 23–36 kg (50–80 lb)	2–4	110–225 g (4–8 oz)	425 ml ($\frac{3}{4}$ pt)
	4–6	225–390 g (8–14 oz)	570 ml (1 pt)
	6–9	390–560 g (14–20 oz)	570 ml (1 pt)
Giant: over 36 kg (80 lb)	2–4	170–335 g (6–12 oz)	570 ml (1 pt)
	4–6	335–560 g (12–20 oz)	855 ml ($1\frac{1}{2}$ pt)
	6–9	560 g+ (20 oz+)	855 ml ($1\frac{1}{2}$ pt)

Add an equal *weight* of biscuit meal or other appropriate cereal to meat (weighed when raw)

Milk This should be considered as a food rather than as a drink. By the age of 6 months, when milk and cereal meals are discontinued, milk should be offered separately. Avoid giving a puppy very cold milk taken straight from a refrigerator.

Housing

The need for privacy Every puppy should be allocated a place of its own where it can be territorial and have some privacy away from the family. Fortunate puppies will have one place in the house and a kennel or outhouse in the garden.

If a puppy is to grow up with a happy lack of neurotic behaviour traits such as chewing its own paws, and howling and barking when alone, this privacy is of paramount importance. No puppy should be left alone all day while the family is out, but quiet periods alone are beneficial. The family must accept this fact, and avoid disturbing and overstimulating the puppy just because it is new and appealing.

In the house it is difficult to find a place that is exclusively the puppy's domain, but the puppy bed must be put in a relatively undisturbed place, free of draughts but also away from any direct source of heat. Sometimes a conservatory is suitable, but beware of overheating in summer.

Safety Before a new puppy is introduced into the family, it is worth considering what hazards it will face around the house, and what precautions may be taken.

Puppies are exceedingly curious about their environment and given to exploring it thoroughly – of course they must, if they are to learn. They are also very active and, like babies, put everything to the mouth. Such ordinary household items as pans of boiling water or hot fat, live cables, toxic cleaners such as bleach, weedkillers, tablets and so on, are therefore all potential death-traps and, as such, must be kept well out of reach.

The puppy's bed In the early days it is necessary to ensure that the puppy actually sleeps in its bed. Certainly for the first few nights a new puppy will be likely to try to stop you from leaving it alone. Resist the temptation to allow the puppy into your own room: it is bad training for the puppy and there is always the risk that fleas (which any puppy may have) will breed in your bedding (p. 29).

A very suitable puppy bed is illustrated. Made of rigid plastic, it is available in a range of sizes and is relatively inexpensive, light, washable, waterproof, and reasonably resistant to the puppy's destructive skills. It is meant to be used with soft, disposable or washable bedding.

The traditional dog basket made of woven willow is not suitable for most puppies which would simply unravel it. Neither are 'bean bag' beds or foam bags suitable. Most young puppies would chew these and would risk swallowing pieces of the filling.

Garden kennel A suitable kennel is illustrated. It should be lifted off the ground about 10 cm/4 in; the roof should be pitched to shed rain and snow; the front should be hinged to open up as a pair of doors for easy cleaning; and the entrance should be at the front, to avoid a draughty bed, not at the gable end.

If the size is right, and if the kennel is well constructed, weatherproof, damp-proof, and furnished with a good bed and warm bedding, then there is no need for concern about the puppy's welfare. With few exceptions, puppies are hardy, and those which live outside permanently grow a thick, protective winter coat (p. 20). The one thing to avoid is subjecting a puppy to wild fluctuations in temperature.

Playpen Many owners find it very convenient to use a playpen to contain a young puppy at night and for periods during the day. A child's playpen can be adapted with the addition of wire mesh or weld mesh, and for as long as it contains the puppy safely, the playpen can be used outdoors or in the house.

Flooring Until the puppy has learnt bladder control, its playpen will obviously have to stand on a washable floor when in the house. It is very important to clean the floor thoroughly when mopping up after accidents, in order to remove the puppy's own odour from the spot. If this is not done, the puppy will continue to urinate and defecate in the same place.

Use newspapers on the floor to help in the house-training of small puppies (p. 22).

Playthings The puppy derives great pleasure from a big marrow bone, but offer only a raw beef shin bone. It is a natural plaything, cleans the teeth, helps in the shedding of the milk teeth, exercises the jaws and provides some calcium. Never give a puppy small bones that may break or splinter, and also beware of a puppy swallowing excessive amounts of powder-fine but indissoluble fragments from cooked bones. Dog chews are a good substitute and certainly less hazardous. As such, many veterinary surgeons recommend that these be given to puppies in preference to bones.

There is a wide variety of puppy toys available. Choose with care and avoid those which mimic personal possessions – such as slippers – too closely, or it will hardly be surprising if the puppy makes the mistake of thinking all slippers are playthings.

Irish Wolfhound bitch and puppies

Maltese bitch and puppies

Golden Retrievers

Basset Hounds

German Shepherd Dog

erriers

Pembroke Corgis

Exercise

Young puppies expend enormous amounts of energy in play, and between their periods of frantic activity should be left to sleep a great deal, undisturbed by children or the household routine.

Their only outdoor playground during the first months of life is the garden, which must surely be a source of great pleasure to them after the restrictions imposed on them in the house. It may be near impossible to make a garden puppy-proof, but part of it must be enclosed if the puppy is to enjoy some play in the fresh air.

During these early months puppies need to be kept away from other dogs, and even away from places where other dogs may have been, in order to minimize the risk of their contracting disease by cross-infection before their own vaccination regime (p. 24) has had time to give them immunity. This need for caution means that going out for even short walks is impossible before the puppy is at least 14 weeks old.

As the puppy matures, it will need to be accustomed to wearing a collar and being held on a leash. Try putting the collar on the puppy for short periods – perhaps before feeding, so that the pleasure of the meal will overcome the aversion to wearing a collar – until it is accepted without fuss. Next introduce the puppy to the leash; fix it on to the collar for short periods until the puppy becomes used to that too. Only then can you attempt to take the puppy out in order to encourage it to walk on a leash, but it is unlikely to be ready for any training on the leash until it is nearly 6 months old (pp. 22–3).

It soon becomes obvious just how much exercise is needed by the big, boisterous breeds such as the Irish Setter, and by the strong, steady breeds such as the Labrador. Increase the exercise programme gradually until, at maturity, the most energetic dogs are having perhaps 16 km/10 miles a day, as well as plenty of freedom in an enclosed garden. A distance of 1.5 km/1 mile is likely to be enough for the smallest breeds.

Collars
Short-nosed puppies such as Pekingese and Pugs will be safer and more comfortable in a harness. Long-necked breeds will be more comfortable in a broad collar. Avoid using chain collars on long-haired breeds which are better suited to rolled collars.

A safely enclosed garden allows a puppy to enjoy some play in the fresh air

Grooming

Grooming is always necessary, and not just for good looks. It removes debris such as dust, dead skin, loose hairs and burrs; prevents serious tangling and matting; massages the skin and improves muscle tone; reveals parasites and other problems; and almost certainly gives the puppy a sense of wellbeing.

The amount of grooming needed by a particular puppy will depend on its coat type, but some daily attention should be given to all puppies to accustom them to being handled and examined. Those puppies which will need extensive grooming throughout life must learn to accept it as part of their daily routine.

Dandy brush

Long-haired puppies
Many people find long-haired puppies particularly attractive. There are many mongrels and crossbreds with long coats, as well as pedigree puppies such as the Chow Chow, Rough Collie, Setters, Maltese, Old English Sheepdog, Pekingese, Pomeranian, Poodles, Golden Retriever, Shetland Sheepdog, Shih Tzu and Yorkshire Terrier.

Brushing, combing and stripping   If a long coat is to be kept in top condition, it is obligatory to brush and comb it daily to remove the loose hair. Another advantage of daily grooming is that carpets and household furnishings are kept relatively free of puppy hair. Unless preparing for the show bench (when special grooming techniques may be used), brush and comb in the direction the fur grows, and pay particular attention to the feathering on limbs and tail.

Grooming mitt

In more natural conditions, the coat thickens up for the winter and moults for the summer. One major factor nowadays is that most puppies are kept too warm and as a result moult throughout the year. The use of a saw-toothed stripping comb will help remove loose hairs, and stripping is particularly desirable in summer when heavy-coated breeds may suffer from excessive heat.

Towel

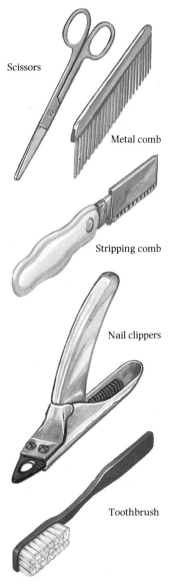

Scissors

Metal comb

Stripping comb

Nail clippers

Toothbrush

Short- and wire-haired breeds

Short-haired breeds such as the Boxer, Dalmatian, Greyhound, Pug and Whippet may be brushed or groomed with a rough mitt. The wire-haired terrier breeds, including the Airedale, Fox, Scottish, Sealyham and West Highland White, need grooming with a very stiff brush and metal comb. Daily grooming is desirable, even if brief. Many terriers also benefit from being stripped in summer.

Bathing

Bathing is not usually recommended for puppies under 6 months of age. If necessary, in unusual circumstances, use a proprietary shampoo and rinse off each application thoroughly. Towel dry and finish drying with a hairdryer.

Oral hygiene

All puppies benefit from being accustomed to having their teeth cleaned with a toothbrush and water from an early age. Regular cleaning helps prevent the build-up of plaque and, when they are a little older, tartar. If tartar deposits accumulate, the result will be receding gums, loosened teeth and very bad breath. Puppies most at risk are those of the short-faced and toy breeds which inevitably have overcrowded teeth.

Clipping and trimming

Puppies such as Poodles and some terrier breeds which need clipping should be taken to a pet beauty parlour for professional attention, at least in the early months. Some owners will become adept at giving a simple trim after they have seen it demonstrated a few times.

Owners of long-haired puppies should use scissors to trim hair between the digits to prevent it becoming uncomfortably matted, and around the anus to prevent matting due to dried faeces.

Nail clipping (p. 10) is not advisable for very young puppies, but may become necessary as they mature.

Basic Training

House-training This should begin in a quiet, unemphatic way as soon as the puppy is brought home. Puppies urinate frequently, and success in house-training depends on anticipating their needs. Regardless of weather, the puppy must be taken outside for a few moments every time on waking, after eating or drinking, etc. Praise or scold gently according to performance. This method is suitable for older and/or larger breeds of puppy.

Small breeds and very young puppies may be paper-trained to urinate and defecate on newspapers spread on the floor. Praise when the papers are used; scold when they are ignored. Gradually move the papers nearer to an outside door and then into the garden before discarding them altogether. Some puppies are house-trained quickly; others take 3 months to learn bladder control.

Most puppies are highly receptive to training and eager to please. However, it is of fundamental importance, when training a puppy, to recognize that the dog is by nature a pack animal and will give its allegiance to the pack leader. In domesticity the owner must assume this role, especially with puppies of the more assertive breeds, or, with minimal opposition, they will assume it for themselves and attempt to dominate the entire household. Calm, firm, consistent and reassuring handling will soon earn their respect.

Simple commands   1. Heel   2. Sit

Training sessions must be very short to begin with, and the puppy must wear a collar and lead so that the handler has control. The RSPCA takes the view that check chains should be reserved for use only with strong, boisterous dogs. If improperly used, the check chain can inflict serious injury to a puppy's delicate larynx and windpipe.

From the age of 6 months, elementary obedience-training classes are recommended. Although elaborate training is inappropriate for pet dogs, a sensible measure of control is vital for safety and enjoyable companionship.

Simple commands From the age of 6 months, certain commands can be taught, such as heel, sit, stay and come. The same word must be used invariably, and it must sound distinct from all the others.

It is important to be consistent in the teaching, to teach only one command at a time, and not to overestimate the puppy's span of concentration. The first lessons should be very brief and so simple that success is all but assured.

Training is achieved by the use of reward and punishment, in the form of praise and scolding. Generous praise should be given for every success, even for a belated success.

Scolding is effective only when instant. It is better to ignore a misdemeanour than to confuse the puppy by scolding later when it is behaving well.

3. Stay

4. Come

Vaccination

Vaccination provides a puppy with protection against certain diseases, so it is important that all puppies should be vaccinated before they start going out for walks, or mixing with other dogs.

Infectious canine diseases

Present-day vaccines give protection against seven serious and relatively common diseases (or disease fractions) in the UK. These are canine distemper (including hardpad), viral hepatitis, parvovirus, two forms of leptospirosis, and both parainfluenza virus and *bordatella bronchiseptica* (each a fraction of the kennel cough complex). Fortunately, it is possible to obtain vaccines which may be used against a combination of diseases simultaneously. Vaccination is very safe and rarely causes an allergic reaction, although the puppy may feel a little drowsy.

The vaccination regime

Most vaccines (but not all) are administered by subcutaneous injection. The usual procedure is for the puppy to receive two injections at an interval of 2 to 4 weeks. The first of these is given at between 8 and 12 weeks of age, according to the risk factors.

Most young puppies from a reliable source will have received some immunity from their dam, by way of antibodies in her milk. When the first injection has to be given early, the presence of these maternal antibodies can interfere with the effectiveness of the vaccination. Any regime, therefore, may need adjusting to suit the needs of an individual puppy. For this reason, advice as to the exact timing of the injections should be sought from a veterinary surgeon as soon as the puppy is acquired.

Vaccines do not give life-long protection and all need boosting at regular intervals: some at 6 months; some after 1 or 2 years. Without these booster injections the degree of protection can fall dangerously low.

Before vaccination, most puppies of healthy dams will have received some immunity by way of maternal antibodies present in her milk. The purpose of vaccination is to stimulate the production of the puppy's own antibodies to combat the various disease organisms. This is achieved either by introducing a vaccine of dead disease organisms which cannot produce the disease but will activate the production of antibodies, or by introducing a live vaccine prepared from a weakened strain of the disease (or a strain which attacks other animals) and which is no threat to the puppy. Again, the result will be the production of the puppy's own antibodies.

In countries where rabies is endemic puppies will also need protection against this most dreaded of diseases; indeed, vaccination may be mandatory. At present the UK is free of rabies and this is due, almost certainly, to strictly enforced quarantine laws which impose heavy fines on anyone found to have imported *any mammal* without submitting it to a full 6 months' quarantine at a Ministry-approved kennels.

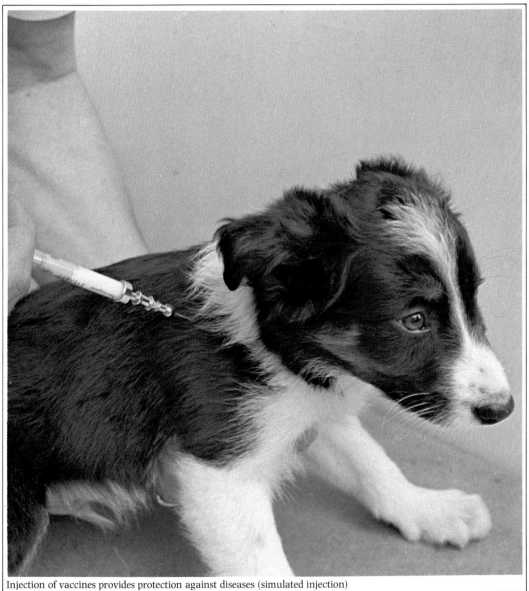

Injection of vaccines provides protection against diseases (simulated injection)

The Healthy Puppy

Abdomen	rounded, not bulging; soft and flexible, not taut or drum-like; not pot-bellied; no swelling around navel.
Anus	clean, with no staining, scouring, or matting by dry faeces; it is normal for puppies to sniff under tails to identify other dogs by anal scent.
Appetite	enthusiastic for food; no undue scavenging; no vomiting.
Breathing	quiet and even when at rest; no laboured breathing; no coughing; normally panting to cool down.
Claws	no splitting; no overgrown claws.
Coat	clean, pleasant-smelling; free from parasites, loose hairs and dirt; soft to the touch, not staring or brittle.
Demeanour	curious, alert, vital; quickly responsive to sounds and calls.
Ears	alert to slightest sound; clean, with no brown or yellow deposits; head and ears held in normal position; no scratching, rubbing or shaking of the head.
Eyes	clear, with no cloudiness of the cornea; not unduly sensitive to light; no discharge or weeping; not bloodshot.
Faeces	consistently formed; colour varying according to diet; should be passed regularly two to four times daily.
Movement	tends to be very active in short spurts with rest periods between; young puppies may sleep 16 out of 24 hours; gambolling, unco-ordinated movement normal; young puppies tend to fall over their own feet; no limping or lameness.
Nose	condition depends upon environment; likely to be cold and damp out of doors, warm and dry indoors; no persistent discharge; nostrils not blocked by dried mucus.
Pads	no matting of hair between the digits due to contamination by mud, tar or grease; no cracked pads.
Skin	loose and supple; clean, without scurf, inflammation, parasites, or sores.
Teeth	clean and white; gums pink except those of the Chow which may show darker pigmentation; shedding of the milk teeth normal (see p. 11).
Urine	straw-coloured, not cloudy; no blood in the urine; passes urine frequently, with no difficulty; both sexes tend to squat to urinate until puberty, when the male begins to 'cock his leg'.

Puppies are generally resilient, happy and inquisitive, displaying the signs of health listed here. When they deviate from these, the owner should seek veterinary advice, initially, perhaps, by telephone. Most veterinary surgeons prefer to see prevaccinated puppies outside normal surgery hours, partly to allow time to discuss such matters as feeding and general care, but also so as not to endanger the puppy by putting it in close proximity to other animals which may carry disease.

Many home cures are suggested as a result of listening to old wives' tales. Do not attempt such cures: do not give old drugs, previously prescribed by a veterinary surgeon; do not give human medicine which, even if appropriate, is likely to be in too concentrated a dose; and do not seek any non-veterinary advice, for instance, from pet shops.

Tablets are often prescribed for puppies by body weight. It is possible to weigh most puppies at home either by using kitchen scales or by standing on bathroom scales holding the puppy, and subtracting the handler's own weight from the scale reading.

Life History

Scientific name	*Canis familiaris*
Gestation period	63 days (approx.)
Litter size	1–6 (small breeds) 5–12 (large breeds)
Birth weight	100 g/$3\frac{1}{2}$ oz – 500 g/1 lb 2 oz
Eyes open	10 days
Weaning age	35–49 days
Weaning weight	1000 g/2 lb 4 oz (small breeds)
Puberty	males 8–12 months females 6–18 months (commonly 8 months)
Adult weight	1000 g/2 lb 4 oz– 70,000 g/150 lb
Best age to breed	males 350+ days females 540+ days
Oestrus (or season)	2 seasons per year
Duration of oestrus	3 weeks
Retire from breeding	males 8 years females 6–8 years
Life expectancy	10–18 years (small dogs usually outlive larger breeds)

Ailments

Diarrhoea   This is a very common complaint in puppies. It may be due to the puppy having eaten unfamiliar or unsuitable food, or to an infection caused by bacteria or parasites. It may on rare occasions be due to an obstruction in the intestine as a result of the puppy having swallowed a stone, marble, or other foreign body. If it persists, or is accompanied by vomiting, veterinary advice should be taken. It may be a symptom of disease and can produce rapid debilitation through dehydration.

Worms   In severe cases, roundworms will be seen in the puppy's faeces, or may be vomited, but even without symptoms, all puppies need to be treated for roundworm infestation. Normally a puppy acquired at 8 weeks of age will have been wormed once by the breeder. It is essential, however, that further worming treatment takes place. Do not attempt home cures, but consult your veterinary surgeon when arranging for the puppy's first vaccination.

Ear mites   A puppy which scratches or rubs its ears, or shakes its head, may have an infestation of ear mites. These parasites feed on the delicate lining of the ear by piercing through the skin. Serum seeps from the wounds to make a characteristic deposit in the ear canal which, in extreme cases, can become completely blocked.

Ear mites can cause intense suffering to a puppy, yet control can be achieved if a prompt veterinary diagnosis is obtained. In neglected cases, the ear drum may be pierced, and permanent middle ear damage can result with such symptoms as loss of balance and convulsions.

Fleas   A puppy which scratches itself furiously may be found to have fleas crawling and occasionally jumping through its fur. These reddish-brown parasites feed by piercing the puppy's skin with their mouthparts and sucking on its blood. Flea droppings, which on examination will be seen in the puppy's coat, are in fact the dark colour of dried blood, containing whole blood cells. There will also be minute clots of blood in the fur, formed when the wounds continue to bleed.

Note on insurance: some routine veterinary treatment is always needed, and its cost must be allowed for when deciding whether or not to take on responsibility for a puppy. In addition, some insurance is advisable to cover unexpected veterinary expenses and/or any legal claim for damages caused by a puppy, for instance, in a road accident. A number of insurance companies design a specific policy for pet owners.

The puncture wounds can become infected, dermatitis may occur, and the flea (as an intermediate host) may transmit tapeworms.

Infestation is most likely in warm weather when the life-cycle of the flea may be as short as 30 days. It is not enough merely to try to eliminate an infestation from the puppy's coat. Control is only successful when it destroys the fleas in their breeding places, notably the puppy's bed and bedding.

Lice An infestation of lice will also make a puppy scratch furiously and frequently. Two species of biting lice and one sucking louse may attack the puppy. The biting lice cannot pierce the skin, but cluster in great numbers around abrasions and at body openings to feed on the natural secretions. Sucking lice pierce the skin to feed. In long-coated puppies it is not easy to see lice. They are small, dull and rather transparent, and tend to cling to the skin. The white nits – or eggs – however, show up well, particularly on a dark coat.

Puppies suffer great discomfort from lice: the sores caused by scratching may become infected; anaemia may be caused by sucking lice; and biting lice (as intermediate hosts) may transmit tapeworms.

The nits hatch in 7–10 days, and the young are mature at about 14 days. Once fertilized, the female lice lay several eggs a day for their entire life of about 30 days. Veterinary help should be sought if lice are suspected.

Motion sickness When travelling by car a high proportion of puppies are affected by motion sickness, with symptoms of nausea, panting and vomiting. The anxiety can also cause diarrhoea. Tranquillizing and anti-motion sickness drugs may be prescribed while the puppy remains prone to such sickness, but most become accustomed to car travel. As soon as the early vaccinations are complete, it helps to take the puppy out in the car twice a day between meal times just for a few minutes at a time.

Responsible Ownership

Under UK law a dog kept as a pet must be licensed on an annual basis. The dog must wear a collar with identification when in the street or any public place, and additional bylaw restrictions make it an offence for a dog to be in certain designated roads unless held on a leash. If a dog causes a road traffic accident, there may be a claim for damages against the owner. The need for insurance is mentioned on p. 28.

Take care to control a puppy when near livestock, particularly for the first time, for many will show an undue interest. It is an offence for any dog to worry livestock, and in the UK it is mandatory for a dog to be on a leash in the vicinity of sheep. Losses are so high that a farmer who shoots a dog found worrying his stock is legally in a very strong position.

In the interest of good neighbourliness, do not allow a puppy to howl and bark when alone. Something has already been said about this habit (pp. 3 and 14), which is the natural reaction to isolation of a puppy unfairly tied up for too long.

The subject of fouling footpaths is now much debated. Ideally, puppies should be trained to defecate in the garden (see p. 22), and the faeces should be disposed of daily. If puppies have to be taken out to defecate, guide them to the gutter and take care to see they do not foul parks, play areas, pavements or footpaths. The American practice of collecting up the faeces is another solution.

The eggs of the dog roundworm *Toxocara canis* are discharged in the faeces. Accidental ingestion of these eggs by children (or adults) can in rare cases cause health problems and even partial loss of sight.

Puppyhood lasts barely a year, yet puppy ownership is the responsibility of a decade, and sometimes nearly two. Early care and training, and the attitudes shown to the puppy when young, will determine whether it is to become a sad misfit and a nuisance to the whole neighbourhood, or a trusted and treasured companion.

Two Red Setter puppies

Index

A
Afghan Hound, 4, 8
Airedale, 4, 9, 21

B
Basset Hound, 4, 9
Bathing, 21
Beagle, 4, 9
Beds and bedding, 14
Bloodhound, 4, 8
Bones, 15
Border Terrier, 4
Borzoi, 4, 8
Boxer, 5, 9, 21
Bull Mastiff, 5, 8
Bulldog, 5, 9, 10

C
Cars, puppies in, 29
Castration, 7
Chihuahua, 5, 8, 9
Chow Chow, 5, 9, 20
Claws, 11
Clipping and trimming, 21
Collars and leash, 18
Collie, 5, 9, 11
Crossbred puppies, 6

D
Dachshund, 9, 10
Dalmatian, 5, 9, 21
Dewclaws, 11
Diarrhoea, 28
Distemper, 24
Dobermann, 5, 8
Docking, of tails, 11

E
Ears, 11, 28
Eyes, 10

F
Feeding, 12–13
Fleas, 28
Fox Terrier, 21

G
Genitalia, 10
German Shepherd Dog, 5,
    8, 10
Golden Retriever, 4, 20
Great Dane, 5, 8, 10
Greyhound, 4, 8, 11, 21
Guard dogs, 5
Gundogs, 4

H
Hardpad, 24
Head, 10
Hepatitis, 24
Hounds, 4
Housing, 14–15

I
Infectious diseases, 24
Insurance, 28
Irish Terrier, 4, 9
Irish Wolfhound, 4, 8

K
Keeshound, 5, 9
Kennel cough complex, 24
Kerry Blue Terrier, 4, 9

L
Labrador Retriever, 4
Lakeland Terrier, 4
Law, puppies and the, 30
Leptospirosis, 24
Lice, 28
Long-haired puppies, 20

M
Maltese, 5, 9, 20
Milk, 12–13
Mites, ear, 28
Mongrel puppies, 6
Moulting, 20

N
Nail clipping, 21
Newfoundland, 5, 8, 10

O
Oestrus, 7
Old English Sheepdog, 5,
    8, 20

P
Papillon, 5, 9
Pekingese, 5, 9, 11, 18, 20
Pembroke Corgi, 10
Pointer, 4, 9
Pomeranian, 5, 9, 20
Poodle, 5, 9, 11, 20, 21
Pug, 5, 9, 11, 18, 21
Pyrenean Mountain Dog,
    5, 8, 11

Q
Quarantine, 24

R
Rabies, 24
Retriever, 4, 9
Rhodesian Ridgeback, 4, 8
Rottweiler, 5, 8
Rough Collie, 20

S
Safety, 14
Saint Bernard, 5, 8
Saluki, 4, 8
Samoyed, 5, 9
Scottish Terrier, 4, 21
Scratching, 28, 29
Sealyham, 21
Setter, 4, 20
Shetland Sheepdog, 5, 9,
    20
Shih Tzu, 5, 9, 20
Short-haired puppies, 21
Siberian Husky, 5
Skye Terrier, 4
Spaniel, 4, 9
Spaying, 7
Stance, 10
Stripping, 20, 21

T
Tail, 11
Teeth, 10, 21
Terriers, 4, 9
Toy dogs, 5, 9
Toys, 15

U
Utility dogs, 5

V
Vaccination, 18, 24
Vomiting, 28

W
Weighing, 26
Welsh Corgi, 5, 9
Welsh Terrier, 4
West Highland Terrier, 4,
    21
Whippet, 9, 21
Working dogs, 5
Worms, 28

Y
Yorkshire Terrier, 5, 8, 9,
    20